At Whatever Front

Sundress Publications • Knoxville, TN

Editor: Erin Elizabeth Smith
Editorial Assistant: Jane Huffman

Colophon: This book is set in Adobe Caslon Pro.

Cover Design: Kristen Ton

Book Design: Erin Elizabeth Smith

At Whatever Front
Les Kay

Acknowledgements

Many thanks to the editors and staff of the following journals, where the following poems previously appeared, sometimes in altered form:

Borderlands: Texas Poetry Review: "Catfish Creek"
Blue Earth Review: "Cloud Formations" and "Summer 1951/2009"
Cellpoems: "Exodus"
Cider Press Review: "Subject to the Logic of Dreams"
East Fork: "Cryptozoology"
edifice WRECKED: "After Dilation, I Am Not Quite Myself" as "Dilation"
Eclipse: A Literary Journal: "Marlene Dietrich on the Radio" and "Google as Memento Mori" as "Googled"
Hermeneutic Chaos Journal: "That First Summer Job"
Jabberwock Review: "Persephone in Southeastern Ohio" as "Persephone"
NonBinary Review: "Andromeda"
PANK: "Another Uncertainty Principle"
Read This: "Career Planning, 1984" and "On the Back Patio of My Wife's Childhood Home, Wintersville, Ohio"
Redactions: "Occasional Fables"
Santa Clara Review: "Das letzte Stilleben"
South Dakota Review: "Losing Blues"
Southern Humanities Review: "Home Front"
Stirring: A Literary Collection: "Portrait of an Artist as a Young Woman"
The McNeese Review: "Footnote (Day of Remembrance)" and "Blood of the Maccabees, Blood of the Gazelle, 1109-1125" as "Blood of the Maccabees, Blood of the Gazelle"
TPQ Online: "Blue Memento"
Uppagus: "Against Reason"
Word Riot: "Methamphetamines"
Wherewithal: "Other People's Exits"
Whiskey Island: "E-4"

Table of Contents

Some Pending Threat

This House, Its Fractured Foundation

At the Edge of Our Knowledge

for Matt

Some Pending Threat

Blue Memento

The warehouse heat seeped
through his shirt, pushed temperature
up like typhoid; pneumatics whirled
and presses clanked steel and wood
with enough force to slam razored
dies into cardboard or an errant hand.
On busy days, his ears hummed
like alarm clocks, his blue uniform
darkened with sweat, fresh paper cuts
remapped the calluses of forty years
with tributaries of blood, and his eyes
blurred with the repetition of movement,
but after each twelve-hour shift, my father
gathered the mistakes which were a fraction
of an inch off and folded the boxes himself,
so that he might have a memento of each
account to display along the shelves
of his trailer, so that he might cradle
baseball card boxes, glazed like enamel,
and hold them out to me saying:
     Look, Son, look.

A Sort of Empire

Studded with plastic painted
to resemble post-war fables
(Rudolph, Frosty, Peppermint Patty),
the Montana house, close enough to
Mount Airy Forest to imagine deer
stopping for eggnog, yields extension-
cord secrets in the unlit afternoon.

Come nightfall tradition, or something
like it, offers simulated snow, long-
shoed elves, candles flickering.

O, Nostalgia! O, Waste! I love you
as you blind uphill drivers. Come
again (and again and again) from Taiwan,
bearing more magic than a Mondrian.
Let lucky children believe a little longer
in that city unto itself, almost golden,
upon a hill, with plastic lit like emerald scarabs,
glass bright as brooches on royal gowns.

O, Excess.
I remember my father driving us
to Highland Park in his Oldsmobile Firenza
to see the executive version of Christmas
given, freely, to children like me
whose parents gave their bodies to warehouses,
shop floors, factory lines
for the luxury of others—so much
light, cascading, almost, everywhere.

Cryptozoology

*– In 2003, anthropologists discovered a
skeleton in a cave on the island of Flores in
Indonesia. Nicknamed "hobbits," the
ancient humanoid averaged three-and-a-
half feet tall and explained, to some, local
tales of the "Ebu Gogo," believed to kidnap
children.*

Mornings before I woke, my father would be up by five,
sitting at the kitchen table, brewing blended coffee,
boiling water, and spreading mustard (was it mayo?)
on sandwich slices of white bread for a baloney lunch.

He would open two paper packets of instant oatmeal,
pour their dried flakes into a bowl dolloped with margarine.
Baptize the concoction in boiling water.

Every workday for fifteen years, this was breakfast.
Lattes were serpentine tales from Scottish lochs.
Hollandaise? As likely as meeting a hobbit for elevenses.
Omelets with ham, rare Sasquatch sightings.

Now, I can't remember a single conversation
we had before he drove twenty miles to cut cardboard all day.
Maybe he told me tall tales about a boar his grandfather

killed with twine, a duck whistle, and a bottle of whiskey.
Maybe he sketched the long comedy of the spring toboggan ride
outside Fairbanks that snapped his Air Force-issued glasses
into snow-melting monocles I sometimes imagine perched

on the snouts of upwardly mobile wolves. Maybe he sang
the smallest saga, set in Dallas, of his first bookbinding months
in an open shop, the strike that almost brought the union in,

or the day they went back to work without union cards.
Most days, though, he knew I wasn't ready to listen.
He'd let me float through the ocean of sleep, spotting narwhals
and megamouth sharks from a bathysphere of bunched blankets.

Since then, I've seen a skeleton of *Homo floresiensis*.
I've dreamed hobbit-like hands reaching for mine.
I've been taken too far from what once was home.

That First Summer Job

We chased cottonmouths
deep into the creeks that
      split the public parks, left
      our chrome bicycles prone
in clay mud along the oak-
lined banks; canopies, green
      as crayons, gave shade to
      our beatings of bush, stone,
earth as if the trees themselves
somehow knew from our cat-
      quick moves and our moth-
      like flight how much our scheme
meant to us, so gave a cloak
of broad, bristling leaves to
      protect our pasty skin from
      the sun's arc as our stories
of what each of us would do
once we caught that critter
      by the neck or by the tail,
      echoed down the creekbed,
and I boasted, as only a boy
could, that I would fling
      my catch into the first black
      Cadillac that passed on the
nearest street, but we never
caught anything more
      venomous than a little oak,
      a cache of bright fire ants,
and, of course, our selves.

Another Uncertainty Principle

In high school, before the slender "s"
of integrals, it seemed simple,
a law that could never be broken:
push and you will be pushed back,
reeling. Equal and opposite.

When friction was added, my math
became a mess: how much force
to a wrist pressed into an Adam's apple?
For a stolen video game?
A snap kick to the groin?

With more complex interactions,
I got lost in vectors: a roundhouse
kick's parabola, a knee shattering
in gravel, an angle for escape,
another. The reactions lacked
the predictability of a child's punch:
insult his mother, brace yourself.

I guess I couldn't fathom the language
Newton fashioned to explain his world,
so I came back to my tongue: the tip
touches the teeth to make meaning.

Catfish Creek, Texas

We—there is no we—stumble off swamped trails,
concocting tall tales of how the other fell.
But no one falls.
                                    Instead, dogwood blooms
white as dandruff—nothing until you've
seen the same nude tree opening itself
into shyness where rain huddles in want.

Above, stars gather their patterns, a little
dimmer, maybe, not that you could tell:
the Milky Way circles the swamp night's finger.
A wedding band. Alligators stir to the din
of shirtless boys croaking their names,
looking for a fight. Somehow, no one falls.
Our fists are flowers that we can't open.

Ms. Thompson Discovers Delta, Colorado

Drawn by promises still carved
beneath the bleachers of any small town

football field, she left her family,
her city, her state behind

for mountain pass and possibility;
she held his muttered words like a stent

until she gave all she had to the infant
that defied physician statistics,

forsook lives she felt that epiphanic
fall when colors, like a biblical coat,

seemed to tell the tacking of unseen hands
over valleys. Now, those same leaves conceal

voles, wolves. There is no language in land—
only the cross-stitch of seams holding

together across boulder currents,
hook-thick streams, two-lane highways.

Elsewheres, like the taste of currant jam,
lead her home to her mother's rental,

to a city of skyscrapers and railroads,
to the endless planning of the unplanned.

Portrait of an Artist as a Young Woman

As when you imagine yourself
an opossum treed by domesticated dogs,
waiting with bared teeth as seemingly solid
branches crack beneath your feet, lightening
your pouch, all that you carried with you,
so to the dawn, when ideations of a better life
ally themselves with dust-covered notions
of politics—fragments from your own personal
Precambrian period—and you wonder
what it is you have to offer, how long you
can continue to hiss away leaping dogs,
the distance between now and when
night is taken from you, and whether anyone
has heard the circling,
                              so to the blank pages,
your own riverrun, silversilent in moonlight,
a clutch of broken branches, a song.

Theories of Ghosts

His watch ticks, stutters like a dull-blade plough.
Hands tremble with a rubric of despair.
He waits for signs the world is not a snare,
an unsprung trap. Faces on a black bough
(jigsaws to be solved) taunt like a dare,
like lines on a palm. Fragments (tufts of hair
from a father, dead before birth) cohere
in visions that scatter like pavement ants
into peeling cracks of plaster. Speculation
(a man breaks the dirt, a drought breaks the man)
half-clog gaps like a lover's unskilled hands
smearing mortar into shattered foundations.
On the platform, bright petals (a passing glance):
a dragonfly alights; a lily opens.

Exodus

Cirrus whispers
splotch sky.

A C-5 severs
form, space—

fruit fly,
half-finished canvas.

Wind lifts scraps of news:
bombs in Jerusalem, baseball.

Career Planning, 1984

In Safeway, a boy in a black cap slips
quarters into slots to buy new lives.
The boy loops his bomber past pixel tracers
from digital MiGs, pounding his fingers
numb on red buttons. A burst of flack
grazes the wing, and his money is done.

Outside, a swept-wing B-1 banks above
suburban rooftops, trembling lace curtains.
The Lancer touches down behind razor
wire, searing rubber into tarmac as it
screeches to a halt.
                           For a better view
of the base where his best friend's father
loads bombs into the black bellies of jets,
he scales a dogwood, blooming cloud-white.

This House, Its Fractured Foundation

Footnote (Day of Remembrance)

When a fighting man dies,
they say the diminutive daisy
sprouts from spilled blood.

In French, they call it
immortelle sanguine.
The Hebrew translates
to "Blood of the Maccabees."

Bible stories. (Fighting men,
dead.) "Red Everlasting."
So many names for that flower.

Once, I heard it told
in another tongue—
"Blood of the Gazelle."

I search now and again
but find only English,
Latin, French, Hebrew.

The blooms, as red as
albino blackbird eyes,
know no borders.

We pin them to our chests,
drawing blood,
drawing blood.

Blood of the Maccabees, Blood of the Gazelle, 1109-1125

– a ghazal in several voices (from trader to caliph)

Word reached me as I wandered from Antioch
to Acre to trade pepper with the Franks again.

When our father joins the unseen world, we're brothers
who turn our swords upon each other again.

Your letter, like the poisoned wells of Jerusalem,
wrapped my path around an unquenched thirst again.

Our own caliph slept outside the city's stone walls,
ordered them razed for the Romans, left us again.

Even here, where donkeys refuse their packs, and rain
is scarce as wine, red blossoms skirt our path again.

Red Everlasting

She thought herself born for farewells,
for serving blood sausage to the courtesans
of the cardinal who'd swayed her brothers
to take the cross and sail toward morning—
just as her father had on the eve of her fifth year.

Properly averting her eyes, she waited
in the bishop's house for her brothers
to return from the Holy Land, taking solace
in whispers with the steward about the bishop's
manners until the steward cast her name aside.

Her brothers returned only in piecemeal:
in the slant of an infant's cheek, the lilt
of a girl's laugh, the ravings of a beggar
trading tales for alms: battlefields with blossoms
like talons clutched around a quiet heart.

Pale of Settlement

Here in the distance,
      beyond the pale,

where Catherine's line
      of demarcation, porous as
winter skin, drapes
      across a frozen land—

useless as an infant fist—
      hearth plumes seed
the city's freezing fog
      and slick frost is all

that is left of earth. Nothing,
      save callous rumors of life,
remains: a prayer book
      tucked in the pocket

of a tattered coat braces
      a boy against a wind fierce
as history's whims.
      He walks the shtetl's alleys,

murmuring fragments,
      inventing a permeable Kiev.

Das letzte Stilleben

As Klee hoped for a convalescence that never
came, news of another European war crackled
through exile radio, filled the Swiss press with
speeches, movements. If, then, the black
background seemed to him to spread in a single
plane, with the rapidity of an idea, beyond the
taut lines of canvas into his cluttered studio, into
the ticking streets and over the Alps, into the
mined fields where children in camouflage and
khaki charged, like him, into their death, and if
there was no dawn to wait for, no window to
escape through, he left, at least, color: beneath a
burnished tea kettle, lines of fallen wildflowers
wait to be gathered, a fertility statuette at their
side. A small portrait, the color of concrete
(with shades of rose) tilts upward in the
foreground. The figure, with bare feet, is large
for its frame, distended across multiple planes,
as if conflicted with itself. It clutches its fists, as
if the gesture were enough to mask downcast
eyes. A collection of vases—muted azure, sandy
taupe, sepia, and verdigris—draw the eye away.
All, save one, wait for flowers to fill their
mouths. Roses (I will call them) bloom above
the lip of the other. And in the center of the
canvas, a gamboge disc—sun, moon, or
incandescent bulb—hovers between kettle and
vase, offering its own light.

Marlene Dietrich on the Radio

Lyrics held falsetto
linger in the larynx

and syntax dissolves
to pitch and tone.

Relics from behind barbed
fences clutter the kitchen:

a sepia photo,
creased faces, catalogued

forearms, etched forever
with concertina wire;

a dingy medal, clipped
from its tricolor ribbon;

letters from a fiancée
on her endless way to France.

Home Front

I. November, 1967

She worried the slow erosion of speech
like whiskey eating stomach lining,
tying up all her tongues with barbed wire,
but he made her speak again, twittering
nightjar song against another threat
of war.
          If a heart knows anything at all,
she thought, *it knows the possibilities of plot:*
love unfurling like banana leaves after
a long night's frost.
                 And yet, William's kiss—
blown across an open palm as his
troop ship, leaving for Southeast Asia,
sailed beneath the good-luck banner
she and six other families had hoisted
over Golden Gate railing—nestled
like habit into reflection's rigmarole.

II.

O, those tender years, our modern Thebes,
incapable of knowing guilt. Onward,
where others, folded into rugged ice,
wept crystalline tears over eyes whose
frozen sheaths shattered now and then
like the cathedrals tended in those
tropics of our first wanting selves.

III. March, 1968

Pools of water prismed blacktop.
A snail's shell popped beneath her shoe.
The count was four. Four cracks
of exoskeleton. Four amniotic blobs
adhered to the soles of her favorite shoes.

The rain slowed its unholy pace.
Mist laminated the streets
the way flora's thirst was quelled
before the deluge, before Noah
compressed creation between
bow and stern.

At home, she peeled off soaked socks,
hung them across the shower bar.
Sat to massage her feet,
peeled white with wet.

She put on a favorite record,
but even Coltrane's take on Rodgers
& Hammerstein would not solo
high enough to warm the wet room.

The pine floor stuck to her soles.
Goosebumps rose like braille
across her skin.

Will I see those four snails in some inferno,
she wondered, *still struggling across concrete?*

Weather filtered to marrow,
crept up her spine. Fever claimed
life in the jungles of the world

while she waited for the letter

that never arrived.

IV.

Uneven bedsprings, distended—she
clung to patchwork quilt, handsewn.
His grandmother. In that half shack,
half dream, what did she say? Spitting
distance from the Red River. Alarm
clocks. Cathedral bells. Alarm bells.
Cathedral clocks. Bells, bells. Alarm.
William in a neighbor's wheat field.
Bells, bells, bells. Air-raid alarm.
Holding a sunflower head, her heart,
the size of cathedral bells. Air-raid.
Bells, bells, bells. Air-raid cathedrals.
A half-glimpsed life. *He loves me not.*
Petals falling from wheat-chafed hands.
He loves me. Bells. Alarm. Telegram.

V. June, 1968

Steel wings threw
him into the air. STOP
He rose until the world's
ceiling shattered hands. STOP
Impact. STOP

He expected the mingling
of wind and silk. STOP
He expected wings
outstretched like a condor's. STOP

He fell toward terraced
fields of rice. STOP

Persephone in Southeastern Ohio

After sundown, her father would
bounce her on his knee, threatening
always to tilt her into the oblivion

of hardwood floors, but pulling
her back into his arms just as she felt
her ponytail trail across the boards.

She told me once how he had
arrived that April at Dachau,
propping his rifle against a bruised

shoulder, hoping like hell he could
shower soon, scrub the blisters
from the heels of his feet.

She couldn't say, as we sat swilling
espresso, much of what he told her,
only that his eyes sometimes fixed

on the eastern horizon as if he expected
to see that brick chimney billowing
thick smoke into sky, bodies piled

like kindling, blinking skeletons
whose names were taken, lost again.

Summer 1951/2009

The wind, a breath, arcs
budding treetops into ballerinas:
plié   jeté   pirouette
and in one half-open attic window
among these houses that were,
not so long ago, identical, a lace curtain
undulates as if a ghost were pulling back
the shade, peering out at the altered world:
the goldenrod fire hydrant, the listing
telephone poles, the children driving by
in Japanese cars. I know (of course)
that movement is no more than wind,
but I let the attic phantom wander
the unfinished floors, as if up from
a midsummer nap torn with flashes
from the Philippines (jungle thick
with stinging blindness of sweat).
How happy he must be, must have been,
to look out the attic window at his wife's
sun hat bobbing like a coconut
in an island current as she studies,
or studied, a sapling oak, preening
and pruning with new shears.

Her Radiation (Tulsa), His (Khafji)

How could she
explain the way they

changed: the echo of his
words tilting like parasols

in typhoon, his remembered
smile crackling her Geiger-

counter nerves, the photographic
fold of his pressed, desert

arms exhuming desire
she'd been told to bury?

She was lonely as a guitar.
Distortion followed

footsteps. With her ballooning
belly, she waited.

E-4

Mother never saw, but he dangled
scaled-down soldiers with white yarn,
imagining their cheeks bulging like

puffer fish, until neck bones broke,
but nothing would last; he raised
unfortunates for another assault,

barbed their bodies at whatever front.
He froze their plastic skin next to ground
beef for Salisbury steak where they would

sweat like cold soda cans in summer,
but frostbite never blackened molded
fingers; they too would stand clutching

plastic grease guns at the next battle scene—
until that year his father came back,
drove north past the state line where red-

and-yellow highway-side stands offer
firecrackers for the Fourth with little
thought to children's eyes or hands.

That weekend at the lake, one soldier
clutched the wheel of an armored jeep
as spark traveled fuse to a bundle of black

cats, jumping jacks. Superglue might
have brought the soldier back, but that
was the closest—until the sweltering

December he stood hour after hour
outside Fallujah waving sand-scarred
trucks through the checkpoint until

a corporal under his command shouted
halt! in English instead of Farsi—

By her last tour in Kandahar Province

she began to read minds—
watching the twitch of a too-tight cheek muscle
flit across transient faces—
faces that felt sadder than trying to call
home with a cracked satellite phone,
sadder than never smelling autumn again,
sadder than a Florida malamute in August—.

Thoughts were vapor.
Meanings swarmed as she spoke—
legionary ants lugging a gecko's
carcass to colony and queen.

The land—a spirochete—
bored beneath her skin,
fevering everything,
even what was left still of her.

Last Chance to Play Lost

A mortar shell struck the shoulder-high wall,
and as the blast of white smoke and ash
cleared, Lance Corporal Thompson was over
the edge into canyon, thousands of feet
below the camouflage while tracers filled
the sky like fireflies as we—why was
I there?—huddled against what was left
of precipice edge, stone.
                      With no plan, no
rope for rappelling to Thompson's aid,
no whirlybird near, no path to reach,
his buddies leapt into the crevasse to meet him—
one after another and another. First
went Jenson who had filled the empty
hours talking with Thompson about
fly fishing outside Colorado Springs.
Then went Leszek and Guerrero, trying
to roll the force of their bodies from the fall
into stone, dust, and sod.
                    Then, when none
of the others moved, Jackson went as well.
Fireflies buzzed our heads until he stirred,
minutes later, and stood, wobbling like
he had on the night of his last leave, then stooped
to tend to Thompson's wounds: gashes, limbs cracked
and snapped like kindling. Friends, like their
chattel, scattered across the canyon floor—

I woke with sweat in my own queen-sized bed.
I woke to maybe now I know something—
slight as sunbeam mites—of the wars
our fathers fought by following brothers, thin

43

as winter, beyond strictures of logic
into abyss. They knew: love is and does.

Sergeant Jenson Considers Ceaseless War

I.

The shoppers wander, rush from store to store,
festooned with plastic and paper bags
as bright as opium poppies in sun-
drunken fields outside Lashkar Gah, in search
of the perfect products to keep their children
from complaining on Christmas Day—too much.
Scarf-masked faces garish as lightning bugs
(to Sergeant Jenson) collect more and more
to stack beneath their trees while he scans their
growing listlessness for signs of something
not quite right. His gaze washes over rings
that glint like sun on an autumn stream where
trout leap. His gaze pours over cashmere coats
almost as black as his son's first self-portrait.

II.

His gaze only fixes when he spots what
could be to him a weed among the poppies:
a boy who's dressed the way his son once was;
a girl who looks like his neighbor's daughter;
a man whose coat shows signs of wear, like his;
a woman with eyes slow as muddy water
like his wife Caroline's. He copies
the time and place into his notebook, watches
the every move of those unlucky few,
pausing only after they leave the mall
or are caught enough to warrant a call
to those whose orders he aches to eschew.
Or when performed courtesies make him pull
his hand from his holster to tip his hat,

Good morning, Sir.

III.

At lunchtime, he retreats to the food court
as those he watches over swarm like wasps
to blossom, flitting between sushi stands,
taquerías. Sometimes, after he
has finished his PBJ or chopped ham,
he nods off and almost drifts into a sleep
where he is a boy floating among waste
until ribbons and tissue paper part
beneath a stolen dinghy's bow. The river
opens to pure tributaries that their
bruxing voices cannot reach, where
his son returns a while from forever
for one last holiday to wade with him
and fish the familiar shallows of Blue River.

IV.

He can almost feel the tall tales begin
to spin from cracked lips—of double shifts,
flustered white women lost without their phones,
celebrity shoplifters, terrorist plots
he foiled while writing up a parking fine.
He can almost hear his son's laugh, soft
as a cattail seed head, calling bullshit
before his son tells his own tall tales:
tranquil strolls through the sands and fields
of Helmand Province. He longs to listen,
to hold his tongue as the river before them
rises up, giving trout to casts that fold
the sky in half, a second horizon,
almost, then back to watching what's bought, sold.

At the Edge of Our Knowledge

For Ruby

Sleeping off annual shots in the spare room,
she howls out of her sleep, letting her lungs
empty of fear to stave off some pending
threat beyond what my ears can manage.
I think for a moment that the strained waves
of her canine voice could ricochet
the bedroom walls without dissipating,
like so much sadness:
                                    A silver bicycle
stolen outside a corner store, a one-eyed
doll buckled in the backseat of a rental car,
a first rose tucked within the seventh canto
of *Paradiso*.
                        Her howls, I think, could float
from this house, its fractured foundation,
its teardrop eaves, slip through the chimney
with winter's first fire, up into cloud,
into ozone, into the Van Allen belt,
into a star's captive debris, into the spiral
ancients imagined as milk, into the furious
torsion at the center of what seems everything,
into the emptiness beyond that, until it
happens across other howls, other songs
at the edge of our knowledge where quasars twist
upon themselves,
                            but I'm tired, too tired
to believe the sine and cosine of her sudden fear
won't cease its oscillations of molecules
when space becomes too much nothing, so I
lie down beside her, letting my fingers search
the crevices between her flopping ears
and the cowlicks that dot her collared neck

as we curl together, overlapping,
and I tell her it will be all right, not
because I'm sure, not because I believe
it's true, but because it helps her sleep.

Against Reason

Although my veranda was nothing more
than cobblestone tile
wrapped with window screens
to prevent the perseverance of mosquitoes,

we sat there, as if it were a resort, sipping mojitos,
watching parakeets flit
between mango trees,
when your son Seth mentioned that the king

of France is bald, and we toasted
him *in absentia*
before the rain
interrupted our revelry—like dementia disrupting

the give of love after decades, leaving the take behind.
We dashed inside
and perched beside a window
to watch the sky fill with lightning and count

toward the crescendo of summer's first thunder.
We gazed out
at avocado trees,
their blossoms, clustered suns orbiting

the *Mangifera*, when the rain ceased its beating
of palm fronds,
and the mangos burst
into a sunlit song before we could see they

were parakeets fluttered with wet, darting
from branch to branch.

Losing Blues

A crow weaves hair into its nest. It caws
as if quoting phrases from your hymnal,

still kept where photos rot in our closet.
Carpenter ants scavenge the cupboard shelves,

swarming, when light flickers on, like pixels
on a television that's lost its signal.

Without you, the apartment bares itself.
Mangoes fester. I clutch the hymnal

you left behind and think of last year
when we picnicked on the coffee table,

and the house geckos and boat-tailed grackles
perched together on your shoulder and hissed

for the pumpkin cherries you held as you
stroked luminescence, like dew, from their backs.

After Dilation, I Am Not Quite Myself

The optometrist sends me home
with frameless plastic sunglasses.
I weep wasp stings. Pools of rain

drown my footsteps, and cars
ooze into an amorphous mass
of blue. Traffic migration snaps

with a wreck. Air bags blow
to embrace the bodies, muffle
impact. A woman, I think,

stumbles from mangled fabric,
glass, and steel cacti, raises
a hand to her head. The wind

lashes her clotting hair, patterns
palms across crabgrass—greener
as one bleeds into the other.

Google as Memento Mori

Life is a series
of disconnections:
the lure of orchards
bending with fat citrus
severs our temporary bond;

I have not forgotten
your taste: black sand
and brine; salty
tequila.

This is the tenuous
thread of difference,
a cast of shadows, the sun
breaking through sea.

I know this, at least:
our lives are bountiful
in their loss and
this is beauty.

Methamphetamines

Alone, stranded at six o'clock,
some guy asked to borrow my pen
to ink his index finger with a cross.

I handed it to him without a thought;
then, he shouted about some woman,
alone, stranded at six o'clock,

waiting for him in a coffee shop.
I feigned concern for that cracked man,
inking his index finger with a cross.

As he spoke, he drew a watch
across his right wrist, its hour hand
static, stranded at six o'clock.

*This ring of red and gold came off
only once, and she left me then.*
He inked his index finger with a cross.

At last the train had reached my stop;
I rushed for the stairs and left him
alone, stranded at six o'clock,
inking his index finger with a cross.

The Bird People

I.

I cheated on a lover once. It's tough,
years after she last pressed her swan skin
against me, not to twist the truth
like twigs and twine in a magpie's nest.

I'd like to tell you I was spotted
by an owl-shaped man who tracked
me from a rooftop perch.
I'd like to tell you the other woman
taught me to feather my skin, cleave
to contours, each updraft of wind.

II.

Somewhere, they imagine better lives
for themselves: sorghum sways, alfalfa
stalks bend, corn ears thicken. Elsewhere,
pigeons fatten at drive-thru trash cans.

I'd like to tell you no more secrets
remain, that love, like the unsteady
V of migrating geese, falling in line,
will take us where we need,
but maybe you've not forgiven me.
Desire—a murder of crows, narrative
scavenger—picks carrion clean.

III.

When I told her what I'd done,
I didn't think about us. But all
of us. All of us wanting with
gaping beaks, all of us charting
flight paths, deep as weather,
into the corners of ourselves
where trash cans are always

full, where we strive to ignore
all the others that glut the skies
we want torn open for ourselves.

Occasional Fables

Then, change was the only constant in our lives.
Children still rode skateboards down rickety
sidewalks, flew kites beneath black power lines,
and danced themselves muddy in summer storms,
but they were someone else's children. Others,
whose laughter scored that drunken portion of
our lives, have left the cold smokestacks behind.
One man spends nights scanning hybrid roses
for signs of aphids. Another studies supply
and demand on a corner downtown, and masters
marketing in a day-glow jumpsuit.
And one woman performs in films
she prays her parents never see, though Mother
already knows. Another directs foot
traffic through Samarra streets, honing new
language with commands that infect his sleep.

Then there was the girl whose sole
aim was to follow the dictums, stricter
than the codes that keep skyscrapers aloft,
of her own erratic conscience. We hear
reports of her now and again, finagling
loans from fed-up friends, taking day jobs
with immigrants, selling heirloom tomatoes
at the apogee of a Montreal blizzard.
Rumors spread, honeysuckle in unkempt lawns.
One neighbor even claims to have spotted
her pulling a man three times her size
from the torrential New Orleans streets
into a canoe. She had wrapped him
in a blue blanket, covering his face,
as a mother would, so the cameras would not

see his tears. He says that man's body had
shook as she held him. Most, though, believe
she is in hospital somewhere, weaving
stories from the few truths she's learned to trust,
letting plots arc and fold, but never arrive.

Andromeda

dog-ears a second-hand
copy of *Stranger in a Strange
Land*, remembers ten years ago,
when she slid into silk chemise,
letting it cling to her skin
like a studied dream of time travel.

Her songs blasted through torn speakers.
Eyes turned up in supplication,
and she started to sway, as slow
as star death, holding each captured gaze
hostage on an alien world.

She would strut for them, peel off her
long gloves, her Lycra gown, broadcast
her thoughts like a telepath so
everyone knew that if the world were
without envy, she would stay the night,
charting spiral galaxies,
on the small of every back.

                    Now her bass line
is pneumatic blades cutting cardstock,
laminate, which she stacks into
cardboard boxes. She works through lunch—
pausing only to bandage cuts—
all to make a paltry piecemeal
bonus and keep her rent current.

Each night, her hands and wrists sting, ache
as if she had spent the day chained
to ocean rock. Some nights, she gives

herself to television's sea.
Some nights, she stretches across the bent
springs of her tweed sofa, becomes
her own Perseus, remembers

the trick to watching yourself
as if from afar, from another
planet, circling another star
in another galaxy, where Earth,
everyone, is but the wobble
in a dim light, a shoulder, wing.

Subject to the Logic of Dreams

Although this may sound like a gin-soaked line,
last night, I dreamt about you and your coal

overcoat in the festooned Neon of Manhattan.
Wind swirled flakes of autumnal snow up

from gutters. Kanji, flashing amber, emerald,
and cherry framed your face. So what if you

were, moments later, someone else? We walked
that city block, our footsteps falling in

common time across gum-crusted concrete
I've never seen,
                      and then the dogs, wanting

out, leapt into our bed. I hurried them
into the yard while trying hard not to wake

my wife, and stood on the stoop, lacing narrative
to the logic of dream: your sudden absence, coat

tattered, a path in the City, unchanged.
From the porch, the fresh-cut grass, heavy with dew

in streetlamp glare: millions of tenements
cascading light across a tiny island.

Main and Fourth

Through the swelling, she smiles when you sign in.
You ask, *how are you?*

                     I'm ok, she says,
and you nod, then ride the elevator
up into cubicles overlooking
the Ohio. You'd think you'd remember
something like that—the off-color of bruise
wrapped like a parka's hood around her
left eye, the way the soft silver dangling
from her earlobes struggled to pull your gaze,
the way her thickened lips crimsoned with work-
week lipstick—but it doesn't take long
to forget, to sink into some business
for a VP of offshoring, to check
the score from last night's Bengals' game, to let
yourself think (only for a moment) maybe
she deserved it, because you can't shake
the idea that sometimes people, people
like you, do deserve it, and if she did,
there would be no more speculation
about whether it was some random act
of violence, a red light run, a fall down
a flight of stairs, or precisely what you
think it was. The problem would be solved,
there would be no need of explanation,
no reason needed, but for a while
you forget, and then at lunch, you walk past
the security desk, and outside,
a man crosses traffic against the light,
mumbling to himself, throwing stares,
like stilettos, at every passerby,
until he comes to you, and the police

ride by on bicycles, as you wait for
someone, anyone, to be taken
the fuck away, but no one is, until
you return to work, walking past her desk,
and you nod, and she smiles again, she fucking
smiles, slowly, as if the effort aches.
And maybe this time, you deserved it.

Cloud Formations

Great Britain sulks across starlight
through the channel. Betelgeuse, blinking

orange, appears where ships have sunk
with Dover in sight. A north wind

drowns cicadas as Europe approaches.
I have work to do; banks need semicolons,

precise use of passive voice, bullets
made parallel, and "products" capitalized.

Later, the island will empty itself of rain
over the cornfields of Southern Indiana,

and punctuation shall be set free
to marauder down empty streets,

making sentences from what's left of night—

Several Small Epiphanies

Lemon poppy seed
muffins. Vanilla bean
coffee. Forgot to eat,
almost fell last night.

Never forgot to eat
as a child. Fried baloney.
Chopped ham. Privilege
is the chance to forget.

Storytelling runs,
like large frontal lobes,
in families. Profit, like love,
begins *in medias res*.

Origins have been malleable,
re-envisioned: mangers,
wicker, rivers, birthmarks,
exile. Benign, malignant.

Pressed flowers framed
above a bassinet. White
and violet blankets bunched
to cover a ceramic doll.

Tungsten in a cell phone.
Poppies in politics. Children
in hunger. I meant a larger
family. You know, Eve's.

On the Back Patio of My Wife's Childhood Home, Wintersville, Ohio

The first fall mist shaded the valley's shrubbery
as tenants and landlords stirred from Sunday sleep.
It seemed as if no one—not even mockingbirds—
had yet woke; the sun, even, lazed in autumnal repose.

That's when I spotted the startled doe,
sniffing plastic cemetery flowers,
and her half-sized fawn, slow as mist.

Let's say what seemed was real, that a soporific
haze of precipitate had spread, like an idea,
across Hanoi nights and Baghdad afternoons,
that no one else, save us three, had stirred,
for they, mother and kid, seemed to know
we were alone. They twitched their slick
black noses as if to measure the differences
I posed—aftershave, toothpaste, flatulence,
all pungent with something that must have been
half-known—then broke their gazes
and shot into the valley where I dared not follow.

I do not know how long I stood there
studying an absent horizon before a light
plane flew overhead, and the mockingbirds,
at last, quavered cardinal tones, but it was,
surely, not as long as it seemed.

Other People's Exits

I tried to tell you,

as my eyes scanned the shoulder
of another interstate for frozen deer
and speed traps, and our dogs rummaged
through their terrier dreams, twitching tiny legs
as if burrowing for remembered moles
into pillows lined along the backseat,

that togetherness,

and the music you chose to frame our midnight
as we veered past other people's exits,

*is an act of agreed
upon composition—*

country homes bejeweled with aluminum roosters,
hunting stands tucked in ash groves,
truck stops selling refurbished laptops and chicken marsala,
dim chapels overlooking fields of sun-chafed alfalfa.

Outside Chenoweth, we missed the HELL IS REAL
billboard, its crimson H, but still you quipped,

*like a saxophone player
blasting a line over, through
a familiar riff*

We call it Chenoweth. In Columbus,
I ran wild with the dogs through yellow
grass, and waiting, you bought antacid.

And then, as we sped down another
interstate, *We're just a pair of headlights,*
you said, *halfway home like everyone else,*
weaving through ten thousand other songs,
the ten thousand midnights they frame.

Poem for My Son

Clichés are bamboo shoots beneath your
fingernails, the cacophonous swirl
of tongues that measure tone differently
than that upon which we've built a life
and the lives of others. They

are machetes cutting permafrost.
Yet, here they are, compounding interest
on unpaid debts: first word your mother
recognized as word, first quivering
step, first song sung, first song sung

where pitch is no longer mistaken
for volume, first day filled by others,
your tiny back bowed by that too-big,
Cobra backpack. They are malamutes
tracking capybara and

ocelots through the Amazon brush.
This wasn't the plan. Almost there, we
thought plastic Saturdays at Circuit
City, Don Pablo's, Border's, K-Mart.
Almost there—just a touch more

time, a few more grains of sand, really:
stop smoking, tidy up the office,
finish this damned book, then pen a life-
changing Tuscan villa novel, but
we had you named and assumed

you would announce yourself as sickness,
accident. We waited on small dogs,

almost ready, when everything changed,
everywhere. I lost my job and your
mother lost hers. Houses where

poodles had yipped lost Chevrolets, Schwinns,
sofas, windows. Our neighbor, a food
truck chef who never mowed his own lawn,
was replaced by an aluminum
For Sale sign. We could not conceive

you then without changing assumptions
we could not change. Here they are again:
history is written by winters,
life should have no fare, the early bird
gets batted by the neighbor's

free-range calico, friendship is stiff
drinks, dinner out, and French manicures.
I worry about her—the woman
who would have been your mom. She takes care
of me, of the dogs who dwell

with us in your stead—Andrew, we would
have called you. This is, is not: first kiss
missed, first job at Burger King, first car,
bruised as a thrice-dropped apple. Andrew,
figment of commonplace, meme,

and cliché, would that you were there in
that someplace of reading, so that I
could tell you this or that, for we are
not the only ones who gave up, give
up, bamboo shoots, tones on tongues,

machetes, malamutes, tidy up,
stand up. I love you, my son—my son

that never was, my aporia
of who I thought I was and would be—
forgive me, us, everyone.

Notes

"Portrait of an Artist as a Young Woman" owes an enormous debt to James Joyce and my wife.

"Exodus" mentions the "C-5," which is a military cargo plane, the C-5 Galaxy, manufactured by Lockheed. Its first flight was in 1968, and the plane remains in regular and reserve service.

"Blood of the Maccabees, Blood of the Gazelle, 1109-1125" attempts a glimpse at the "crusades" from a non-Western European perspective. For more about the history of the crusades, see Thomas F. Madden's *The New Concise History of the Crusades*.

The "Pale of Settlement" was an area of Imperial Russia to which Jews were confined that was established by Catherine the Great. Even within the Pale of Settlement, Jews were forbidden from living in major cities such as Kiev. Moreover, the concentration of Jewish people made the Pale particularly susceptible to pogroms across Russian history.

"Das letzte Stilleben" translates literally as "The Last Still Life." Paul Klee's son catalogued the 1940 painting under this title.

"Home Front" is inspired, in part, by a poem written by Ho Chi Minh, in part, by a conversation with an American veteran of the Vietnam War, and, in part, by Dante's *Inferno*.

"E-4" takes its title from the fourth enlisted rank for men and women in the United States military. For example, in the Army, an E-4 rank would be a corporal or a specialist. In the Marines, the rank would be a corporal.

"Last Chance to Play Lost" is a common American military euphemism for Lance Corporal (LCPL), an enlisted rank in the U.S. Marines.

"Against Reason" uses the phrase "The king of France is bald." That phrase, which Bertrand Russell first used in his 1905 essay "On Denoting," is a proposition of questionable truth value that was important to Russell's theory of descriptions and his defense of that linguistic theory.

"Poem for My Son" mentions several national chains. All of those chains filed for bankruptcy as a result of the "Great Recession."

Thanks

Thanks, first, to my wife, Michelle for being my first reader and my most constant supporter. Next, thanks to Matt Egan, whose friendship and intellect had a profound impact on the early shape of this book and much of its content. Thanks are also due to my father for not only being an ardent supporter of my work and life, but also for allowing and encouraging me to write about his work. Thanks also to the many teachers I've had, particularly John Balaban, Don Bogen, Marcus Cafagña, Fred D'Aguiar, Jim Daniels, Danielle Cadena Deulen, and John Drury.

Thanks also to the many peers and friends who saw portions of this book or an iteration of this book in manuscript form: Eric Bliman, Brian Brodeur, Ellen Elder, Micki Myers, T. A. Noonan, and Linwood Rumney. And of course thanks to my editor, Erin Elizabeth Smith, for pushing me and the book.

About the Author

Les Kay is the author of the chapbooks *The Bureau* (Sundress Publications, 2015) and *Badass* (Lucky Bastard Press, 2015) as well as a co-author of the chapbook *Heart Radicals* (ELJ Publications, 2016). His poetry has appeared widely in journals such as *The Collagist, Redactions, South Dakota Review, Southern Humanities Review, Sugar House Review, Whiskey Island,* and *The White Review.* He is also an Associate Editor for *Stirring: A Literary Collection.* He currently lives in Cincinnati with his wife, Michelle, and two small dogs. Learn more at leskay.com.

Other Sundress Titles

Theater of Parts
M. Mack
$15

Every Love Story is an Apocalypse Story
Donna Vorreyer
$14

Ha Ha Ha Thump
Amorak Huey
$14

major characters in minor films
Kristy Bowen
$14

Hallelujah for the Ghosties
Melanie Jordan
$14

When I Wake It Will Be Forever
Virginia Smith Rice
$14

A House of Many Windows
Donna Vorreyer
$14

The Old Cities
Marcel Brouwers
$14

Like a Fish
Daniel Crocker
$14

Suites for the Modern Dancer
Jill Khoury
$15

What Will Keep Us Alive
Kristin LaTour
$14

Stationed Near the Gateway
Margaret Bashaar
$14

Confluence
Sandra Marchetti
$14

Fortress
Kristina Marie Darling
$14

The Lost Animals
David Cazden
 $14

The Hardship Post
Jehanne Dubrow
$14

One Perfect Bird
Letitia Trent
$14

The Bone Folders
T.A. Noonan
$14

CPSIA information can be obtained
at www.ICGtesting.com
Printed in the USA
FSOW02n0553051016
25667FS